TEEN SUICIDE

Is It Too Painful to Grow Up?

Eleanor Ayer

Twenty-First Century Books

A Division of Henry Holt and Company
New York

Twenty-First Century Books
A division of Henry Holt and Company, Inc.
115 West 18th Street
New York, New York 10011

Henry Holt® and colophon are registered trademarks of Henry Holt and Company, Inc.
Publishers since 1866

Published in Canada by Fitzhenry & Whiteside Ltd.
91 Granton Drive, Richmond Hill, Ontario L4B 2N5

Printed in Mexico

Created and produced in association with Blackbirch Graphics, Inc.

Library of Congress Cataloging-in-Publication Data

Ayer, Eleanor H.
    Teen Suicide / Eleanor Ayer. — 1st ed.
        p.   cm. — (Issues of our time)
    Summary: Describes the victims of teen suicide, the warning signs, the grief of the survivors, and means of prevention.
    ISBN 0-8050-2573-1
    1. Teen Suicide—Suicidal behavior—Juvenile literature. 2. Suicide—Prevention—Juvenile literature. [1. Suicide.] I. Title. II. Series.
HV6545.9.A94   1993
362.2'87'0835—dc20
                                                                       92-35742
                                                                     CIP
                                                                      AC

Contents

A Permanent Solution to a Temporary Problem

Teen suicide takes the lives of thousands of America's youth each year. And with every year that goes by, the problem becomes worse. According to *The Universal Almanac*, teen suicide almost tripled between 1950 and 1990. Today, suicide is the second leading cause of death among American teenagers, after accidents. Some experts say that suicide would be the number one killer if the truth were known about many of the "accidents."

Each year, nearly 5,000 young people choose to end their lives. Twenty times that number attempt suicide but are unsuccessful. Many, many more suicides go unreported. A teenage boy dies from a gunshot wound, but his parents

Wreckage is all that remains after one of Tennessee's worst car crashes. It is widely believed that many automobile accidents are actually unreported suicide attempts.

refuse to admit that their son committed suicide. His death is reported as an accident. A teenage girl is killed in a car crash, but she left no suicide note, so her death is listed as a highway fatality. Police estimate that one quarter of all teenage highway deaths are actually suicides.

Teen vs. Adult Suicide

What is different about teen suicide? The teenage years are a time of many difficult changes. Adolescents are not yet adults, but they are no longer children. They still need parental support, but they also want to be independent. Many teenagers feel that their families do not understand them. They rebel against parental control. This struggle is a difficult but normal part of growing up.

For some teenagers, this turmoil turns to anger. They want to rebel against adults who are in control. But rather than hurting or hating their parents or elders, these troubled teenagers turn their anger inward. They hurt themselves instead, by turning to suicide.

The reasons behind adult and teenage suicide are often different. Many adults who kill themselves have an illness from which they will never recover. They choose suicide rather than years of pain and suffering. Other adults are very sad and lonely after

The Teen-Suicide Epidemic

The number of teens who kill themselves has increased greatly since World War II. Forty years ago, suicide was fourth on the list of causes of death among teenagers. But from 1950 to 1980, the rate nearly tripled. A former director of the National Institute of Mental Health (NIMH) says we are "in the midst of an epidemic of adolescent suicide." Another NIMH official calls suicide "the public health problem of the 1990s."

Why are more and more teenagers taking their lives? The increase in suicide is tied to various problems in our society. Drug and alcohol use have increased tremendously in the last 30 years. Today, nearly 20 percent of all teenagers are problem drinkers. About the same percentage—nearly 12 million people under age 18—have mental-health problems. Youth today are under much more pressure to succeed socially, academically, and athletically than they were 30 years ago. Failure, or fear of failure, makes them turn all too often to suicide.

Family life has changed in recent years. In many homes, Mom no longer stays at home with the kids. Mom and Dad are both out working, so children are put in day-care centers or left to care for themselves. Children often become loners when there is no adult at home with whom they can talk.

Today, more than 3 in 10 children are involved in a divorce. Many other youngsters are abandoned by their fathers. Millions of American homes have either a stepfather or no father at all. Young people from broken homes often feel that they have no one who cares, nowhere to turn, and, as a result, they resort to suicide.

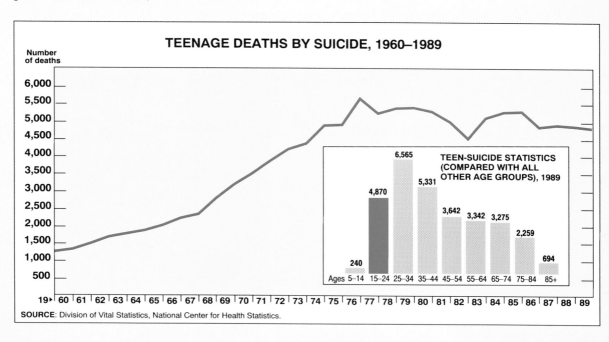

TEENAGE DEATHS BY SUICIDE, 1960–1989

TEEN-SUICIDE STATISTICS (COMPARED WITH ALL OTHER AGE GROUPS), 1989

SOURCE: Division of Vital Statistics, National Center for Health Statistics.

the death of a husband or wife. Seeing no hope for the future, they end their own lives.

Experts tell us that adult suicides are frequently planned months, sometimes years, in advance. But young people often act without thinking. A single, triggering event occurs after a run of bad luck or a period of depression, and within minutes or hours a teenager attempts suicide. Adults are less likely to act so hastily.

Fortunately, many suicides fail. Why? Psychiatrists believe that many teenagers who attempt to kill themselves do not really want to succeed. Their attempts are actually cries for help, warnings that they are in trouble. Dr. Thomas Caffrey is a New York psychologist who counsels suicidal people on the telephone. "Five minutes of my time is spent much more effectively with a teenager than with an older person. In that short time, a young person will listen and begin to respond to help. With an older person, it can take an hour or more."

Experts say that young people often have a hard time understanding that death is permanent. Some teenagers see suicide as a glamorous way of drawing attention to themselves, like a heroic scene in a sad movie. Unfortunately, teenagers forget that the movie is over in two hours, but suicide is forever. Adults, because they have had more experience with death, can better understand its permanence.

The Power
of Suggestion
Young people are often easily influenced by the suggestions, ideas, and actions of others. A newspaper story or television report about suicide can strongly affect a troubled youth.

Jessica had been unhappy for a long time. It had been rough at the middle school, and the thought of going to a larger high school seemed impossible. She simply could not shake her unhappiness. One night, Jessica learned that a 15-year-old girl in a nearby town had killed herself.

Two days later, Jessica was dead. Did the news report push her to commit suicide? Yes and no. The idea of suicide was not new to Jessica. She had thought about it before. But in her unhappy state of mind, perhaps the news of the other girl's suicide was all it took to push Jessica over the edge.

Some people say that exposure to suicide in news reports, music, and movies persuades more teenagers to try it. The director of an Illinois mental-health association disagrees, however. "All in all, the press coverage has helped," she says. "It's much better to get this out in the open."

Does this mean that we should talk about suicide with young people? Yes, say the experts. Open discussion at home and at school about suicide and death can be one of the best ways of helping a suicidal person through difficult times.

The heavy-metal rock group Judas Priest performs at a concert in Houston, Texas. Controversy still remains over whether or not some heavy-metal lyrics promote suicidal behavior.

Can Music Make You Do It?

Straightforward talk about suicide will not encourage a person to try it, most experts believe. But it took a $6.2 million lawsuit to decide if the words in heavy-metal music had influenced two young Nevada men to kill themselves.

Ray Belknap, 18, and Jay Vance, 20, had spent a late-December afternoon in 1985 listening to the music of Judas Priest, a popular British rock group. After nearly six hours of music, beer, and marijuana, Jay later told police, "All of a sudden we got a suicide message, and we got tired of life." The two were listening to a song called "Beyond the Realms of Death." Part of the song says, "He couldn't take any more./Keep the world with all its sin./It's not fit for living in."

"I more or less believed the answer to life was death," Jay said. "So we did the suicide pact. Ray was in the same frame of mind that I was.... And we got the same burst of energy at the same time. That "energy" led Ray to head for a nearby school playground, where he put the muzzle of a shotgun into his chin and pulled the trigger.

Bound by their pact, Jay picked up the gun that was lying nearby, set it against the merry-go-round, and then counted to 30. "My whole life flashed before my eyes. My mother, my father.... I thought about Ray, who was already gone. I don't know how long I stood there, a minute, two minutes...."

Then Jay pulled the trigger. But instead of hitting his brain, the bullet simply tore his face apart. For three long years, Jay suffered from his injuries, finally dying of an apparent overdose of the drugs prescribed for his pain. But before he died, Jay wrote a letter to Ray's mother. In it he said, "I believe that alcohol and heavy-metal music, such as Judas Priest, led us to be mesmerized."

Ray's mother filed a lawsuit against Judas Priest and its production company, CBS Records. Shortly after her son's death, she said she had found the Judas Priest album, "Stained Class," on his stereo. Although she later admitted, "I couldn't understand it. Not a word," she based her case on two words from the song "Better by You, Better Than Me." The two words were: "Do it." Just *what* exactly listeners were supposed to do was not made clear.

Soon Jay's family joined Ray's in the suit. Their lawyer argued that if a person is considering suicide, the "do it" line would strengthen the urge. He based his case on the album's "subliminal messages." These messages can't be understood through the words. They are said to appeal to the subconscious mind, causing people to respond to the music in ways that they would not otherwise.

The group's guitarist was shocked by this. "Nothing in the album says, 'Go do this, go do that,'" he claimed. Apparently, Judge Jerry Carr Whitehead agreed. He ruled in favor of Judas Priest and against the parents. The music, he believed, had not been responsible for the young men's actions.

2

......

Suicide: Who Tries It and Why?

Psychologists say there is no such thing as a "typical" suicidal personality. Most teen suicides are committed by white males from middle-class or upper-middle-class homes. The suicide rate for whites is nearly twice as high as it is for nonwhites. Yet, statistics say that African Americans attempt suicide more often than people of other races. They simply do not succeed as often. Among Native American youths, the number of suicides has tripled during the last 20 years.

While there may be no "typical" suicidal personality, experts say victims do share some common traits:

Low self-esteem. People who feel good about themselves—their ability to succeed, their

A teenage girl stands alone, excluded from the peer group behind her. Many depressed teenagers who commit suicide feel alone and isolated.

personality, the way they look—have high self-esteem. But those who have a negative opinion of who they are—dislike themselves, think they have no place or purpose in the world, feel inferior to others—have low self-esteem. Often there is no basis for low self-esteem. Talented, good-looking, kind, intelligent people often suffer from it.

Loneliness. Not surprisingly, lonely people are among the highest risks for suicide. Loneliness is a feeling of not being accepted by others, whether by one's classmates, one's parents, or other adults. Some teenagers isolate themselves with drugs or alcohol. Some have a disability or are made to feel different for religious or racial reasons. Some just never form close friendships.

Difficulty expressing emotions. People who can let off steam easily when under stress generally are not those who attempt suicide. Instead, it is the person who lets anger or sorrow build up inside, the one who is afraid to cry when he or she is sad, who is in danger. Teenagers who are unable to express their feelings often think of themselves as being emotionally dead, which leads to thoughts of being physically dead as well.

Easily angered. Some teenagers become angry easily and are quick to fight. These people lack self-control. It is hard for them to react calmly or logically in a difficult situation.

Success Does Not Always Mean Happiness

February 12 had been marked on Spencer Stevens's calendar for nearly a year. That was the day of the regional finals. Top skiers at this event would go into training for Olympic competition. For months, Spencer had been worrying and wondering about this day.

A tall, blond 17-year-old, Spencer was one of those guys who just seemed to have it all—good grades, a steady girl, lots of friends, and now a chance to ski among the best of the best in the world. That is why no one could believe the news report of January 31. Spencer Stevens was lying in a coma. He had hit a tree while skiing down an intermediate run. The ski patrol that had rescued him called the accident impossible. An expert skier would not have lost control under those conditions. No one seemed to have an answer. No one except Spencer, who now hung near death.

From the outside, Spencer Stevens seemed always to be smiling. But on the inside lurked loneliness, depression, and an overwhelming fear of failure. His good looks, his good grades, his great athletic ability only covered up a teenager in turmoil.

Spencer loved and hated ski competitions. As long as he did well at meets, he could live with himself. But the fun had long since gone out of skiing. All that was left was tremendous pressure to succeed. He knew that one of these days he would lose, and the thought of it was more than he could bear.

Spencer was one of the most popular kids in his class. Yet, he told himself that no one really knew him—the quiet, lonely fellow who wanted most to go off into the woods with his dog and never come back. No one would ever have believed how unsure Spencer really was of himself and how afraid he was of losing, failing, and doing a bad job.

Spencer's feelings are not uncommon, particularly among popular and successful people. In the past, America has lost many popular stars to suicide. People such as Marilyn Monroe, musician Jimi Hendrix, and comic Freddie Prinze seemed to "have it all." They were rich, talented, and adored by millions. But being admired by others is never a substitute for feeling good about oneself. These unhappy stars are proof that happiness has little to do with wealth or fame.

Jimi Hendrix, a popular rock star of the 1960s, seemed to have it all—money, fame, adoration. Regardless of his apparent success, Hendrix killed himself in 1970 with a drug overdose.

Perfectionism. People should always try to do their best. But if a teenager's need to be perfect is all-consuming, perfectionism is no longer healthy. Often, perfectionists are very intelligent, even gifted teenagers. But they set such high standards for themselves that they are never able to meet them. When they fail, they become frustrated, depressed, and sometimes suicidal.

Pessimism. Is the glass half-full or half-empty? A person whose glass is half-full is an optimist. He or she looks at the world positively and sees chances for success. But a person who perceives the glass as half-empty is a pessimist, like Eeyore in *Winnie the Pooh.* "Good things may happen to other people, but never to me." For pessimists, the world is a trap, waiting to spring its jaws shut. Teenagers who have a pessimistic view of the world are more likely to try suicide. They see little hope for succeeding or for solving their problems.

Depression: The Number One Cause of Suicide

Psychologists say that depression—an overwhelming state of sadness or a feeling of hopelessness—is the root of nearly all teen suicides.

Everyone has bad days or weeks, when nothing seems to go right. No matter how hard we try, problems land on problems like snowflakes in a blizzard. If we can keep a positive outlook and believe that the sun will come out when the storm is over, our lives will eventually straighten out. But for a pessimist, the sun never shines. When problems mount, depression sets in.

Child-development specialists say that a certain amount of depression is common in the teenage years. Hormonal changes in the body can bring on depression without warning. A teenager's growing urge for independence fights against his or her fears of leaving home and facing the world alone. At some point, all teenagers feel that adults, and in particular parents, just don't understand them. When these feelings become extreme, they can lead to loneliness and depression.

Many experts believe that depression is anger turned inward. You are upset with someone, but you cannot let that person know. Perhaps your boyfriend or girlfriend does not show you as much attention as you would like. But you are afraid that if you express this, he or she will laugh at you. You are frustrated that you cannot talk about it. Gradually, your frustration turns to anger. If you want to keep dating, you cannot let your anger show. You begin to turn your anger inward. You punish yourself in little ways, such as not going to a movie you've been wanting to see. The greater

Depressed teens often become antisocial and isolate themselves from their friends and family. Most experts agree that depression is one of the leading causes of suicide among teenagers.

your frustration, the deeper your depression. The depression becomes overwhelming.

Psychiatrists cite certain factors that often lead to depression. Some factors that commonly cause depression among teenagers are:

New surroundings. Moving to a new home, changing schools, going to college, enlisting in the armed forces—these are all major milestones in a person's life. Making new friends and leaving behind favorite places, people, pets, or organizations can be frightening and depressing. For some, such moves may be overwhelming.

Family problems. Adolescence is a common time for family squabbles. Teenagers want and need independence. But sometimes these squabbles become major, ongoing battles without solutions. There is a breakdown in communication between parent and child. The young person often feels misunderstood and unloved—feelings that can lead to severe depression.

Failure. Some family problems are caused by a teenager's feeling of failure. Bad grades in school, poor performance in sports, or a general lack of success can make teenagers see themselves as disappointments to their families. Not meeting up to Mom's or Dad's expectations can be a brutal blow to one's self-esteem. This feeling of failure can push a depressed teenager toward suicide.

Ending a relationship. Whether it is with your boyfriend or girlfriend, or your best friend, the end of a relationship can be terrible. Suddenly, it seems as if your whole world is collapsing. All of your emotions come to the surface at once: anger, hurt pride, sorrow, loneliness, and finally depression. Life may not seem worth living without that special person. More than one third of teenage suicides have been committed over the end of a relationship.

Death. The young-adult years often bring with them a person's first real encounter with death. It may be a grandparent, a favorite aunt or uncle, a parent, or a sibling. Suddenly the teenager is faced with the reality and finality of death—a special person is gone forever. If the relationship was particularly close, the death can be devastating to a teenager. The world grows dark. There seems to be no hope for the future. A severely depressed teenager may decide to join the loved one in death.

Relationships are important parts of our everyday lives. When a relationship ends, a person often experiences intense feelings of both sadness and loss.

The Drug and Alcohol Connection

According to statistics from the National Institute on Alcohol Abuse and Alcoholism, 3.3 million American teenagers, or one out of every nine, are alcoholics. Among youth ages 12 to 17, about 12 percent are regular users of marijuana. That figure more than doubles—to 27.4 percent—among young people ages 18 to 25.

Drugs and alcohol slow down normal body functions. They interfere with motor functions and perception. When the effects of drugs wear off, users can become severely depressed. In an effort to shake off the depression, they consume more, which can lead to drug or alcohol dependence. Users are often people who have little self-control. Drugs and alcohol lower their self-control even

A group of teenagers sits around a table with drugs and alcohol. A very high number of teenage suicides are drug- or alcohol-related.

further, causing them to act impulsively, or without thinking. Impulsive behavior is common among teenagers who attempt suicide.

Nearly half of all young suicide victims used drugs or alcohol just before they died, according to the American Association of Suicidology. But in most cases, death was not caused by an overdose of the drugs or alcohol. It was the result of altered behavior brought on by these substances. Drug and alcohol abuse can increase the desire to hurt oneself. A depressed person who is under such influence is much more likely to attempt suicide than a person who is not.

In addition to triggering suicidal behavior, drug and alcohol abuse may be an instrument of suicide. Thousands of people die each year as a result of long-term drug and alcohol use, which is actually a slow method of suicide. Many more people kill themselves—intentionally or unintentionally—by overdosing on these substances.

Feelings of
Guilt or Shame
The burden of bringing embarrassment or disgrace to one's family can be overpowering. For many teens, the weight is too great to handle.

Katrina's sixteenth birthday was a big affair. Her father, who had a special fondness for his youngest

Many pregnant teenagers are overwhelmed by feelings of shame and guilt. Often, those teenagers feel that their only option is suicide.

daughter, threw a big party for "Little Miss Sweet 16." Relatives and friends came from miles around to wish Katrina well. One month later she was dead, the victim of an overdose of sleeping pills and liquor.

Only Katrina's boyfriend knew the reason. A pregnancy test earlier in the month had been positive. The apple of Daddy's eye could not face telling him she was pregnant. It would bring shame and humiliation on the family. Both Mom and Dad were strong believers in family values and the right to life. Daddy was very active in the local church and a well-known businessman in the city. Ending the pregnancy through abortion was out of the question.

It was all too much. And to make matters worse, the clock was ticking. Already Katrina could feel changes inside her body. Her mind screamed, "Do something, do something." Overpowered by guilt and shame, she turned to what she thought was the only solution: suicide. Katrina is not alone. Nearly one fourth of all teenage girls who attempt suicide are pregnant—or think they are.

The Pressure to Succeed

Some children feel that they are the object of too much attention. Someone is always pressuring them to do well in school, join a new club, be the star of the team. No matter how hard they try, they can never do enough to satisfy their parents, teachers, or coaches.

With every success comes pressure to set new and tougher goals. Getting B's is good, but straight A's would be better. The experts say that parents often want their children to succeed to make up for their own failures in life. If their children are successful, then *they* will finally be successful, too.

Adults are not the only source of pressure on young people. Pressure often comes from other teens. Psychologists tell us that peer pressure— pressure to meet other kids' standards—can lead adolescents to severe emotional breakdowns. Being judged every day by people your own age can create tension. Does my hair look good? Will these new sneakers impress the other guys? Am I hanging out with the right crowd?

Children today feel extraordinary pressure from family and friends to fit in and do well.

Pressure—whatever the source—can be a huge burden to a young person. Often it seems as if there is no way out. Just when you please one person, someone else expects a miracle. When the pressure gets too great, where does a troubled teenager turn? How does he or she find relief? "Many troubled teenagers see death as an attractive alternative to stresses," writes a doctor who is a member of the American Association of Suicidology. "For some, suicide is a way to find peace and escape."

PG: Parental
Guidance Suggested   The suicide rate for
young children is much lower than it is for
teenagers. In 1989, nearly 20 times the number of
young people ages 15 to 24 committed suicide than
did those in the 5-to-14 age group. Many of the
professionals say that young children do not have a
very clear understanding of death and, therefore,
they do not think about suicide in the same way that
teenagers do—as an actual choice that they have.
Yet, children as young as 3 years old have killed
themselves intentionally.

What causes suicidal tendencies in such young
children? Sometimes the reasons are physical. A
child born to a mother who had a disease or did not
receive good health care during pregnancy is at a
higher risk for suicide. Babies who had trouble
breathing for more than an hour at birth show
greater tendencies toward suicide than do other
children.

But most sociologists agree that suicide often has
its roots in the home environment. Children whose
home lives fit one or more of the following patterns
are considered higher risks for suicide:

Two working parents. In homes where both
Mom and Dad work or where either Mom or Dad
is missing, children sometimes do not get as much
attention and love as they need.

Children born to parents who did not really want or expect them. These include babies of teenage parents or older parents who thought their child-rearing days were over.

Families that do not express their feelings, either verbally or physically. Remember the bumper stickers that asked, "Have You Hugged Your Kid Today?" Children who are not hugged or kissed often feel lonely and rejected.

Only children. Kids with no brothers or sisters sometimes lack good social skills.

Social-climber parents. Kids whose parents place great importance on getting rich, buying expensive things, or belonging to the right social clubs do not always get the acceptance they need.

Families on the move. A child who has moved several times and has had to adjust to new houses and friends may become a loner.

Death or divorce. Some children cannot accept divorce or the death of a parent.

Problems in the family. When Dad loses his job, an unmarried sister has a baby, a brother fails at college, or a mentally ill grandmother moves in, there is bound to be upheaval in the family. Some children are overwhelmed by such chaos.

Alcohol and drug abuse. A parent who drinks too much or abuses drugs brings turmoil into the home. Physical or verbal abuse is common.

Suicidal parent. Children with a suicidal parent are more likely to be suicidal themselves. Some experts say it is genetic—an inherited trait. But many others cite the child's home environment as the primary cause of suicidal tendencies and behaviors. Living with a parent who suffers from feelings of insecurity or severe depression greatly influences a child. The child of a suicidal parent may get depressed, and the depression could lead to suicide.

Threatening environment. When a parent uses unusually harsh threats or punishments, the child may grow up in fear, feeling as if the ax is always about to fall.

Rejection. Constant criticism from parents can lead a child to believe that he or she will never live up to their standards. This feeling of not being "good enough" can lead to depression and, possibly, to suicide.

Child abuse. Abuse can be physical, mental, or sexual. When a child is beaten regularly or very severely, this is physical abuse. Saying things that will frighten, embarrass, or cause a child to feel worthless are forms of mental abuse. If a parent or other relative tries to have sexual relations with a child, forces him or her to watch pornographic (X-rated) movies, or touches the child's private parts, it is sexual abuse.

When There Are Just No Reasons

As an African-American male, Todd Robinson was in a lower-risk category for suicide than some other people. According to statistics, on any one day, only five African-American men could be expected to take their own lives. But on July 7, 1987, Todd became one of those five men.

Every teen suicide comes as a shock to the parents. For Todd's mother, it was even more difficult to understand because Todd had appeared to be happy. He was 17 years old, had recently graduated from high school, and was preparing to join the navy. In two weeks he would leave, and he assured his mother that he was very excited about his new adventure.

On the afternoon of his suicide, Todd telephoned his dad to tell him that he was going swimming. He also told his father that he loved him. At four o'clock, however, Mrs. Robinson got a call from a friend of Todd's who had found him lying on his bed with blood in his ears. Without needing to be told any more, the mother knew what had happened. Still, the officer's words rang cold and harsh in her ears, "Mrs. Robinson, I'm sorry. Your son committed suicide. He shot himself in his room."

The frantic mother searched her mind for reasons, but found none. "He had so much to live for," she told herself. In just a few months, when he turned 18, Todd was to receive a trust fund. With the money, he had planned to buy a car. He was happy—he had a good future and a family that loved him. So why? Why?

"I often wish I could say that he was on drugs or mentally ill—anything to have a reason for his death"—his mother mourned. "But there were no answers then. And as I look back upon his life—and upon my own—I find none now."

For some families of suicide victims, there are simply no answers. Even Todd's journal, found days after his funeral, offered little explanation. The entries for the days leading up to his death were all typical of any boy of 17. Only the last one said, "Lately the thought of suicide has crossed my mind. I don't know why. I have a wonderful family and friends. I have an excellent future ahead of me. But I think I'm going to do it. Mom, Dad, don't fall apart."

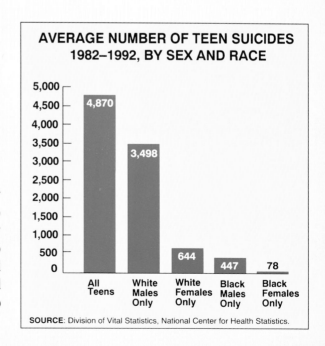

AVERAGE NUMBER OF TEEN SUICIDES 1982–1992, BY SEX AND RACE

All Teens	4,870
White Males Only	3,498
White Females Only	644
Black Males Only	447
Black Females Only	78

SOURCE: Division of Vital Statistics, National Center for Health Statistics.

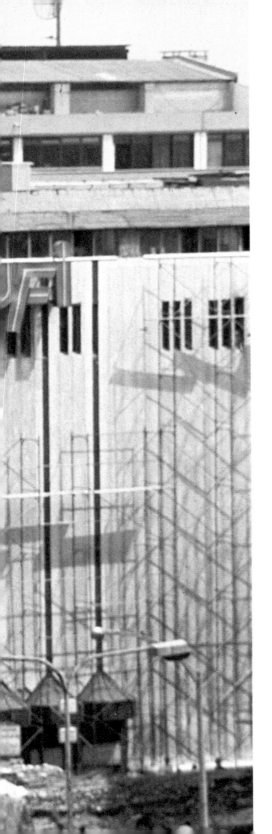

3

......

A Cry for Help

Approximately 1 in every 50 Americans has attempted suicide, and the number grows each year. For every teen suicide carried out, there are 100 to 200 attempted suicides. Therapists and counselors tell us that most teen-suicide attempts are not meant to succeed. These teenagers do not really want to die. They are simply crying out for help.

Jen was a junior in high school when she first attempted suicide. She admits that she had always been a worrier. She worried about how she looked and what other people thought of her. She worried about getting into a good college. In the end, worry overtook her life. "I was so completely out of it, and I really needed

An 18-year-old girl prepares to jump to her death. The teenage suicide rate in the United States continues to rise every year.

help," she admitted. "I just didn't know how to ask for it." She asked in a way that nearly ended her life. Fortunately, those around her listened.

Suicide's Warning Signs

More than 30,000 people a year—nearly 83 a day—kill themselves in the United States. Family and friends are shocked: "We had no idea the situation was that bad." And yet, nearly all suicide victims send out one or more warning signals that should alert the people around them to the seriousness of their situation.

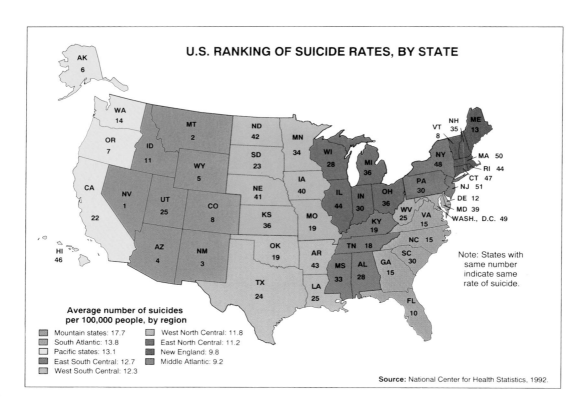

U.S. RANKING OF SUICIDE RATES, BY STATE

Note: States with same number indicate same rate of suicide.

Average number of suicides per 100,000 people, by region

- Mountain states: 17.7
- South Atlantic: 13.8
- Pacific states: 13.1
- East South Central: 12.7
- West South Central: 12.3
- West North Central: 11.8
- East North Central: 11.2
- New England: 9.8
- Middle Atlantic: 9.2

Source: National Center for Health Statistics, 1992.

The following are some common warning signs:

Excessive talk of death. Severely depressed teenagers often dwell on death. They may say things like, "I wonder what it's like to be dead? What happens to your mind when your heart stops?" Often they show great interest in any news story or conversation that involves death.

Threat of suicide. A young person in distress may threaten, "If I don't do well on these finals, I'm going to kill myself." Sometimes the statement is less direct, like, "I wish I'd never been born," or "You'd be better off if I weren't here."

Acting up. It is normal and expected for most teenagers to object to authority. Adolescence is a time for developing independence, for breaking away from parental control. But when a young person is continually wild and unruly, the problem may be more serious.

No concern for personal appearance. Most teenagers want to have clothes, shoes, and hairstyles that are "in." When a teenager cares little about his or her appearance, it could be a way of saying, "Why should I care? I'm no good anyhow."

Lack of interest. If a teenager begins to lose interest in friends, hobbies, sports, or school, he or she may be losing interest in life. Long periods of sitting and staring into space or sleeping during the day can be signs of serious depression.

Getting rid of personal items. When people give away the things that mean the most to them, they may be putting their lives in final order, getting ready for the end.

Prolonged sadness or crying. Extreme moodiness and depression can be signs of a meaningless and empty life. With these moods come tears, silent sobbing, or a continually sad look. Moody teenagers rarely smile and never laugh. Life no longer seems worth living, and their faces show it.

Increased drug or alcohol use. A person who is about to commit suicide may throw all caution to the wind. "What does it matter if I get drunk every night? Soon I won't be here at all." Increased use of drugs and alcohol can be a major warning sign of severe depression and possible suicide.

Change in eating and sleeping habits. Some suicidal teenagers, without realizing it, try to starve themselves. Burdened by severe depression, they seem to care nothing for food. Others eat all the time. Either way, it is a sign of trouble. Another indication of danger is a change in sleeping habits. Some depressed people sleep most of the day, while others have trouble sleeping.

Hurting oneself. Teenagers who are at the point of suicide may first try it on a small scale. In one "accident" after another, they may cut, burn, or injure themselves. These are not really accidents.

Some False Ideas About Suicide

The teen suicide rate has increased a great deal over the last 30 years, but most of us still do not understand the problem clearly. Many ideas about suicide are simply not true:

Only crazy people commit suicide. Some mentally ill people do try to kill themselves. But more often, the attempts are made by healthy people who have become severely depressed.

People who talk about suicide do not actually do it. When teenagers in crisis start talking about suicide, their statements should be taken as serious warnings.

There is a typical suicidal personality. Psychiatrists can draw no single profile of a suicidal person. Some people may be at greater risk than others, depending on their family history, race, or sex, but there is still no predictable victim. Teenagers who attempt suicide include the rich and the poor, blacks and whites, males and females, excellent students and mediocre students.

Talking about suicide will only make a person more likely to try it. The opposite is actually true. *Not* talking about suicide bottles up the depression, loneliness, and fear that are already inside an unstable person. Talking honestly and openly about suicide can bring a troubled person great relief and comfort.

When their minds are made up, there is nothing you can do to stop troubled teenagers from killing themselves. Most teenagers who attempt suicide do not really want to succeed. They simply want someone to pay attention to their cries for help.

Once a person has tried suicide, he or she will not try it again. The sad truth is that four out of every five people who commit suicide have tried to kill themselves earlier, at least one time.

When a suicidal teenager seems happy again, the worry is over. This is the time to watch even more closely. Suicidal teens may *seem* to pull their lives together after a period of depression or an unsuccessful suicide attempt. They may *appear* happy, but their mood is often not real.

Most suicides occur without warning. Most victims have been troubled for some time before they attempt suicide. They are almost certain to show some warning signs.

Every suicide victim leaves a note. Few victims ever leave notes. Many suicides are incorrectly called accidents because a suicide note is never found.

This is self-destructive behavior which, in effect, is an effort to punish oneself.

Physical problems. Some suicidal teenagers can develop physical problems that are not caused by any illness. Such problems, like vomiting every day before school, can be caused by severe depression.

The Straw That
Breaks the Camel's Back

Suicidal teenagers have often been in a state of depression or turmoil for several weeks or months. As pressure builds and stress increases, they creep closer and closer to suicide. But with most victims, it takes one final blow, one last disaster, to push them over the edge.

When Cecilia Lopez's friends looked back, they could see everything much more clearly. During the summer, Cecilia gained a lot of weight. Her friends, embarrassed by her constant munching, no longer bothered to include her in their plans. Soon, Cecilia appeared with a number of bandages stuck to her body. First there was one on her forehead. A few days later, there was one on the palm of her hand and one on her knee. What is going on? the other girls wondered. This just wasn't like her; Cecilia was no clutz.

The reason became clear on December 18. That day, Cecilia Lopez was not in school. Anthony, her boyfriend of many months, was not there either. The news spread like wildfire down the hallways: Cecilia had tried to kill herself the night before. That night, Anthony had told Cecilia that they were through. Losing Anthony had been the final blow for the depressed 17-year-old. All year long, problems had piled up on top of other problems until it seemed as if she could not handle any more.

Had Cecilia's friends been alert, they would have noticed the warning signs of suicide that she had been showing. As things went from bad to worse in her life, Cecilia began to eat a lot. There were more and more "accidents" where she hurt herself. As her depression mounted, she became very moody. Finally, a single event occurred that pushed her over the edge. Feeling that all hope was gone, Cecilia turned to suicide.

Methods of Suicide

Nearly three times more women than men attempt suicide. But nearly four times more men than women actually kill themselves. One reason for this, say experts, is the different methods of suicide used by males and females. Women generally choose less violent, less effective methods of killing themselves than do men. Women are more likely to overdose on drugs than to use guns

When attempting a suicide, a male is more likely than a female to use a firearm, such as a handgun.

or to hang themselves. One reason for this may be that fewer women have access to guns or know how to use them.

Taking narcotics—drugs that cause sleep or that relieve pain—is the method of suicide used most often by teenagers, particularly girls. Sleeping pills and certain other narcotics are often found in household medicine cabinets. Drugs are a less effective method because they take longer to kill a person. If the victim is discovered in time, and if immediate help can be found, he or she may be saved. This is the reason fewer girls die by suicide, although many more of them attempt it.

The second most common method of suicide— and the one most popular with boys—is the use of firearms. Putting a loaded gun to one's head and pulling the trigger is final. Death usually occurs instantly. There is no going back. Rarely is there a chance for the victim to get help. This is why more teenage boys die by suicide than do girls.

Slashing the wrists is another means used by girls. Like taking drugs, bleeding to death is a slow way of dying. If help is nearby, the victim may be saved. Poisonous gas also brings about slow death. Inhaling the carbon monoxide from car exhaust is one such method of teen suicide. Turning on the engine of an automobile that is in a closed garage fills the air with carbon monoxide. This makes the victim sleepy. Again, if help comes in time, the person has a chance of recovery.

Drowning, jumping from a skyscraper or a bridge, and standing in the path of a moving vehicle are all methods of suicide. These methods are used more often by adults. It is difficult to dive into deep water when you cannot swim, or jump off a very high building. Many depressed teenagers are confused and scared about committing suicide. Their uncertainty and fear lead them to choose a method where less courage is required.

Copycat Suicides
Some sociologists say that teen suicide is an epidemic. One teenager commits suicide, and several others follow. Every 105 minutes another person under the age of 25 dies by suicide—that is 13 a day. In one Colorado county alone, 18 young people killed themselves in just 18 months. During a five-week period at an Arkansas high school, 4 boys committed suicide. In New York, New Jersey, Illinois, Texas, and elsewhere, "cluster" suicides have become a tragic new epidemic.

Why does one suicide lead to so many others? Teenagers tend to follow the crowd more than people in other age groups. When a young person commits suicide, he or she is sometimes seen as a hero, one who was not afraid to carry out a threat or

to take "the big step." The desire to imitate the dead person causes other teenagers to follow in a cluster, also known as "copycat" suicides. Often the teenagers in the cluster know *of* each other, even if they are not good friends. And when one person in the group is particularly popular, the number of suicides often increases.

According to sociologists, we "model" ourselves on one another. We find a person we admire or one who thinks as we do, and we try to be more like that person. Teenagers model more often than older people. And so, when one distressed teenager chooses suicide, another may decide to model him or her. The more the teenager identifies with the victim, the more likely he or she is to play copycat. The same is true of a close relationship. A brother, sister, or best friend of the victim is at higher risk for a copycat suicide than a mere acquaintance.

Some people believe that if the media (television, movies, newspapers) would play down these tragic deaths, copycat suicides among teenagers would not be so widespread. While this may sound logical, there is no proof that the media contribute to cluster suicides. In fact, many counselors feel that we should do more to bring suicide out into the open. When teenagers are given the opportunity to talk honestly and directly about suicide, they are not so easily lured by its mystery and intrigue.

Opposite:
A distressed teenager screams in emotional pain as she stands on a rooftop. Frequently, teenagers attempt "copycat" suicides in response to suicides that have already been committed by people they know.

4

Dealing with the Grief: The Survivor's Side

"I still don't believe it," sighed the grieving mother, months after her 19-year-old son hung himself in his college dormitory room. "This kid has me so baffled. How could he have chosen this? He couldn't have been in his right mind. Why he wasn't—that's what drives me crazy. I guess I'll never really know."

The boy's father could not believe it either. "Of all the things I thought I'd have to face in my life, this was not one of them. I always thought that there was a purpose for everything; it was all part of a master scheme. But I will never find an explanation for this."

Randi, the boy's friend, offered an explanation: "Too loving a person, too harsh a world."

Friends of a deceased teenager console one another. The majority of suicide survivors never fully recover from the loss.

Coming to Grips
with Suicide

Shock. Disbelief. A desperate, dead-end search for answers to the impossible question: Why? These are reactions shared by most families and friends of teen-suicide victims. Psychologists estimate that for each teenager who commits suicide, at least six other people's lives are changed forever—for the worse.

Jerry Johnston, who has counseled and lectured on suicide to nearly 3 million teenagers, says this: "The ones you leave behind will never be the same again. Never! They will blame themselves for your self-centered act of final defiance. What's more, if you kill yourself, you may cause a brother or sister or friend to take the same foolish step."

How can the families of suicide victims deal with the death? Johnston urges them to let go—to cry, to talk, to be angry—but not to be silent. "Whenever there is a death in the family, however it was caused, there must be open discussion among the survivors. Without a sharing of hurt, there can be no full healing."

Sadness, hurt, and anger should not be bottled up. Therapists tell us that these feelings are natural reactions to grief. It is normal to cry. It is all right to feel selfish and wonder, "Why did this have to happen to me?" It is okay to be angry and ask, "How could he [she] ruin my life like this?"

Mourners pay their last respects to a teenager lost to suicide. As survivors, they will need to support one another in their state of grief.

Gradually the pain will ease, but the old saying "Time heals all wounds" is often not true for the families and friends of suicide victims. Time and talking about the death can help to dull the pain, but "the hurt never goes away," says the mother of a 15-year-old who died in a cluster suicide. "You start learning to live with it and accept that it's going to be there for the rest of your life."

The father of a 14-year-old victim says he now knows what it is like to be "utterly damned," to live with a burden he will never be able to shake. The pain, the loss, the suffering, and the guilt subside, but they never go away completely. Months or even years after the suicide, feelings of desperation can rush back over survivors and be as intense as they were in the days immediately following the suicide. The anniversary of the death is especially hard. All the events and emotions of that day come back like a nightmare to the relatives and friends who are left to remember the cause of their pain.

Picking Up
the Pieces Although the pain may never go away completely, survivors do find ways to move on. "Human nature is sort of incredible," says the mother of one victim. "We do smile again. We even laugh again. We tell jokes, have a good time. I will survive. But nothing will ever be the same."

At first it just does not seem real to survivors that the person is gone. They still expect to see him or her in all of the usual places. Said one schoolmate, "Every time someone coughed or turned a page behind me, I kept thinking, 'Hey, it's Chris.' It takes a long time for the reality to sink in: 'I'll never see this person again.'"

Finding a purpose in life, a new reason for living, is one of the hardest aspects for survivors to deal with. Jeff, whose 15-year-old friend committed suicide, says that once he was able to think clearly, he realized that life had to go on. "If one person wants to drop out, that's their decision. But you can't stray from your course. There is no good reason to kill yourself. Ever. You can always make a difference in the world."

For the victim's parents, finding new meaning in life is even harder. Raising their child was an important reason for living. With their child gone, their purpose is gone, and they see themselves as failures.

Survivor Guilt

On top of the grief and the hopelessness come feelings of guilt. "What could I have done to prevent this? Should I have acted differently?" Everyone who has known the person shares in the feelings of guilt for the death.

Survivors should remember that it is easier to see things clearly *after* they happen. All those who knew 17-year-old Jeanine carried a burden of guilt for her death. But, said her mother, "We did the best we knew how to do. [Before her death] I didn't have knowledge of certain things.... Maybe if I had had that knowledge, I could have intervened.... We all failed Jeanine in certain ways, but the prime one to fail was Jeanine."

It took a very long time for Jeanine's family and friends to accept that fact—that Jeanine herself had failed. It is difficult to blame the victim. "There are still days," says her mother, "when we don't accept it. We are angry at God, at each other. Sometimes I think we are doing quite all right, and other times I think we are not.... For the most part, we are making a valiant effort to go on."

Dealing with the Pain

Today, one-sixth of all Americans who kill themselves are under the age of 25. In an effort to cope with the grief, survivors are forming a new kind of self-help group. Across the country, centers are reaching out to help families and friends of young suicide victims. Local hospitals often act as gathering points for the groups.

Talking with other people who have lost loved ones to suicide can help survivors ease the pain.

A mother and her children visit the grave of a loved one who committed suicide. Guilt often accompanies the grief that survivors experience.

Hearing how others have handled loss and gone on living can help friends and families pick up the pieces of their own lives. Survivors will often find strength and comfort in talking with those who have been in their situation and can truly understand their feelings.

Survivors are not always limited to friends and family. News of a suicide can shock an entire community or neighborhood. The small town of Sheridan, Arkansas, was shattered by its cluster suicide, when four teenagers killed themselves in a five-week period. The entire community went into mourning. "The school is like a morgue," said one student. "Nobody is talking." Worried parents watched their children carefully, looking for the slightest signs of stress or depression.

At the school, a group called Students Against Suicide was formed. Members of this group got together with a counselor to talk about what had happened. Others preferred to handle the grief alone, in their own way.

It is crucial for an individual, a family, a school, or a community to face their grief. Trying to block out or forget the suicide only makes healing more painful. A high school principal offers this advice: "Don't pretend the suicide did not occur. It is important to express the facts.... In the end, all who are touched by the tragedy will benefit."

The day after a suicide at his school, the principal asked students to take a moment of silence to think about the tragedy and the victim "and consider the alternatives he might have chosen." When students went to the principal's office, he demonstrated a willingness to discuss the suicide but was careful not to paint the victim as a hero. "There is a fine line between sympathy for the survivors...and glorification of the deed. The suicide should not be treated as glorious, heroic, or noble."

There are no policies that tell schools, communities, or individuals how to deal with teen suicide. "None of us understands it," said another principal, "but we do know we must not let survivors believe they are to blame. We must talk with people about the lessons we learn from a tragedy like this. And we must continue to search for answers."

A high school teenager talks with a school guidance counselor. Counselors, ministers, and other adults serve as important resources for depressed teenagers contemplating suicide, and survivors.

Suicide Prevention: How Each of Us Can Help

The suicide rate for teenage boys in the United States is higher than that of any other country in the world. And it is rising. During the last 30 years, the suicide rate for Americans in all age groups has risen by only 11 percent. But among American teenagers, it has increased by 250 percent.

How can we stop this alarming trend? The number-one rule in suicide prevention is "Don't stay silent!" When someone says, "I'm going to kill myself," believe him or her. And don't ever think that this crazy idea will pass. Even if the suicidal person pleads with you not to tell, never promise to keep quiet. Olga, a teenager at Manuel High, decided it was better to have an angry friend than a dead friend.

Teenagers gather to share their feelings and fears with one another. Open communication with trusted friends and family members is a vital part of suicide prevention.

When Sheena, her best friend, announced that she was going to kill herself, Olga's heart started racing. Sheena was serious. She had a definite plan for her suicide and even had a bottle of pills in her pocket.

"Don't you tell a soul," Sheena demanded. "I don't want anyone to know until after it's over. Someone might try to stop me, and I don't want to be stopped."

Olga wanted to scream, cry, and run away, but she managed to stay calm. "Tell me exactly what you're going to do," she urged Sheena. And she listened quietly while Sheena explained to her what she had in mind.

Olga asked Sheena if she had ever thought about what it was like to be dead. The girls discussed it.

Despite her panic, Olga tried to be a good listener. Patiently, she sat while her friend told her about the frustration and depression she had felt over the last few months. When Sheena had finished, Olga said, "I can see why you're so depressed. I'd like to help you work it out."

The girls talked for some time. Then, making an excuse about checking with her mom, Olga went downstairs to use the telephone. In between loud conversations about dinner, Olga whispered into the phone, "Mom, Sheena's going to kill herself. Get help quick."

What Friends
Can Do Sheena was lucky. She had a good friend. Many teenagers who attempt suicide are loners. They think that they have no one to talk to, no one who cares. Very few of them really want to die. They simply want someone to help them.

If you know a person you think is suicidal, do not be embarrassed or afraid to tell someone. Go speak with a school counselor, teacher, religious leader, or other responsible adult. It is always better to do something than to wait.

The experts say that when you are dealing with a very depressed person, it is most important to be a good listener. Try to be understanding. Ask questions that encourage the person to talk. If a suicidal person can tell someone about his or her feelings, it may help to ease the depression. Here are some things to remember:

• Be alert for weapons of self-destruction, such as guns, knives, razors, and pills. Take steps to get them removed.

• Don't be afraid to ask directly, "Are you planning to commit suicide?" This approach is much better than a question like, "You wouldn't really do anything to hurt yourself, would you?"

• If the answer to your straightforward question is yes, do not appear shocked. This could cause the person to lose faith in you as a friend and supporter.

• Never leave a suicidal person alone. Find the time to sit and talk.

• Try not to make the person feel guilty by saying things like, "Think how your parents will feel."

• Don't criticize. "Let's talk about solutions other than suicide" is better than "You're kidding me! You're going to kill yourself just because you're failing math?"

• Don't offer false hope. Shallow promises, like "You'll feel better tomorrow" or "Cheer up—things aren't that bad," show that you don't understand. For a suicidal person, there may be no tomorrow, and things really *are* that bad.

• Reverse psychology doesn't work on a suicidal teenager. If a friend says, "I'm going to commit suicide," don't say, "Yeah, right. Go ahead. I dare you." This may be enough to push the person over the edge.

• Offer comfort, but not advice. Suicidal teenagers do not want to hear what *you* would do in this situation. Even if they ask, most do not intend to follow your suggestions.

• Never swear yourself to secrecy. Do not agree not to tell. When you are dealing with a suicidal person, you need to get help at once, no matter what the person says.

• Don't be too casual. Comments like, "I know how you feel. I've been depressed myself," only

Opposite:
Two friends open up to each other. If a teenager is contemplating suicide, it is important to take him or her seriously, to listen, and to seek out help from an adult.

show a suicidal teen that you do not understand. Unless you have tried to commit suicide yourself, you do not really know how hopeless and unhappy this person feels. You need to let him or her know that you understand how serious the situation really is, without pretending to be an expert.

• Never argue. A suicidal teenager is already at the emotional breaking point. He or she needs a friend, not an enemy—someone who will show caring and understanding.

• Don't ask a depressed person why he or she wants to commit suicide. Instead, listen and try to encourage the person to talk. Then you will know why without asking. Getting the person to talk and being a good listener are two of the best ways a friend or family member can help prevent teen suicide.

What Schools
Can Do
"Schools can't offer long-term therapy," says one psychologist who started a program for suicide prevention. "But they do have an obligation to help troubled kids." Teachers, principals, athletic coaches, and counselors can all play a big part in helping teenagers deal with suicide. Here's what some schools have decided to do:

• Set up a "teacher watch" to identify any students that may be in crisis.

• Provide counseling or psychological help for teenagers who show warning signs of suicide.

• Offer classes on suicide prevention for all grade levels, from elementary through high school.

• Make school a safe, secure, pleasant place, where children *want* to be and where they feel like part of a family.

• Help to build students' self-esteem through classroom work, athletics, and other extracurricular activities.

• Encourage teachers and staff to get to know the children and their families.

Teenagers in Plano, Texas, participate in a discussion group that addresses feelings about stress and suicide. Schools and other community organizations can often help in establishing forums for open discussions among teenagers.

What Troubled Teens Can Do
Schools can help, and friends and family can help. But in the end, it is the troubled teenager who must take the responsibility

for changing his or her life. How can teenagers in crisis turn their lives around?

Many experts say that the most important step in overcoming suicidal feelings is to develop a strong faith. *What* teenagers believe in is not as important as the fact that they do believe in *something*. When things seem to be falling apart around them, some teenagers rely on their faith in God. They believe that if they pray and have faith, God will bring peace back into their lives.

Other troubled teenagers draw strength from a friend or a hero. "Knowing that my brother made it gave me the strength to try harder," said one girl who was 15. "We came out of a bad home, our parents were divorced, but my brother got married and has a good job. I kept telling myself, 'If Joe can do it, so can I.'"

Some teenagers find the strength they need right inside themselves. "I'd really been the route," Stanford admitted. "I'd seen every shrink in town. My parents and I had been through family counseling. I'd spent countless hours in the principal's office. None of it did any good. Finally I realized, 'Hey, dummy, it's you. If you're going to pull through this, you've got to do it on your own.' There were times when I didn't think I could, but I did. And I'm proud of myself now because I relied on Number One."

Stanford discovered another important self-help tool—humor. "I'd heard an old song called 'Been Down So Long, It Looks Like Up to Me.' Every time I'd get depressed, I'd sing a little. Other times I'd laugh at myself, like I'd say, 'Is it really possible for one guy to go without a date this long?' Then, even though it was really hard at first, I'd get tough and force myself to ask a girl out."

Troubled teenagers very often blame their parents. "They wouldn't listen to me if I tried...." "They don't understand me...." "What's the point of talking? It just turns into a lecture." All this may be true, but life is always worth another try. A better route than suicide is to approach a parent calmly. Promise yourself that there will not be an argument. Tell your parent that you are depressed, that you are having serious thoughts of suicide, and that you want one more chance to talk honestly and openly.

The chances are good it will work this time. But if it doesn't, don't panic. Talk to another adult—a friend's parent, a teacher, your boss, or a religious leader. Most people, especially those who know you, will be glad to listen. Do not *assume* that others do not care. Try them. You may be very surprised.

Here's an important rule for teenagers who are in crisis to remember: You are not thinking clearly when you are under stress. After a stressful or

Trained counselors offer advice, support, and referral services to anyone who calls in on a hot line. Hot lines are available for use in almost all communities and are a valuable resource for anyone in crisis.

upsetting event, give yourself several hours to cool off. During that time, find someone with whom you can talk. It may be a person at a suicide hot-line number in your town. If you don't know a local place to call, talk with a counselor at one of the groups that are listed on page 62 of this book. Tell the person that you need help.

For teenagers who find it hard to talk with adults, many communities have suicide-prevention peer groups. These groups are made up of young people in their teens and early twenties. Some have tried suicide. Some have not. All of them are concerned and upset about the teen-suicide trend. They want to help themselves, their friends, and strangers who might be in trouble.

What Gives a Person the Will to Live?

When life seems to have reached its lowest point, why do some people give up and turn to suicide, while others find the strength to go on? Helen Waterford is a survivor of the Auschwitz death camp in Poland, where the Nazis sent millions of people to die during World War II. All around her, Helen saw people being murdered, starved, or worked to death. Many of the prisoners gave up hope under these conditions, and for them death came quickly. But some fought on, despite their situation, and miraculously survived.

Helen and her husband were shipped to Auschwitz in the same cattle train. On the way, he told her that he was sure she would live through this experience and return to their five-year-old daughter. But he was equally sure that he would not. Attitude, how you look at a situation, can influence the way events turn out. "If you make up your mind from the outset that there is no hope, then you lose your will to live," Helen says. She survived. Her husband didn't.

Those prisoners who lived through the death camps had something in common. Each of them had a reason for living. For some, it was a child, a husband, or a wife whom they wanted to see again. Helen was driven by a desire to return to her little girl. Others had a dream, something they wanted to do that kept them going. Helen dreamed of having a small guest house where she would serve elegant meals. "Every night I dreamed about food and how I would prepare it." Even though her dream never came true, it gave her the will to survive.

"My *curiosity* was a great help, too," says Helen. "I always wondered what the next day might bring. Perhaps it would be good. At least it would be different." Even on the train, on the way to Auschwitz, she was curious about what they would see. "We had heard stories about the camps, so we had an idea of what lay ahead. My husband couldn't understand how I could possibly care what we would see. For him it was only bad. But still, I was curious." Her curiosity gave her the will to look to the future.

Occasionally the prisoners were taken out of the camps for delousing, the killing of lice and other bugs that infested their bodies. "Sometimes we would have to stand naked in the cold while they cleaned our clothes and bodies. But at least we were in a different place with new surroundings and people. My curiosity about new situations always gave me the strength to go on to the next day. Those prisoners who had no imagination or curiosity saw no future; for them, nothing was ever interesting."

Having someone you can trust and talk to is very important. In any depressing situation, talking can often give a person hope. But in the camps, Helen remembered, "Some people would simply turn their faces away and refuse to talk. They had given up." No amount of effort by others seemed to change these people's attitudes. They had lost their will to live, and when that happened, death followed quickly. "When this attitude takes over, no one can convince you that you want to live," says Helen. "The desire has to come from within."

Glossary

abortion A method of ending a pregnancy.

adolescent A teenager; a child who is between the ages of 12 and 18.

alternative A choice; a different route or solution.

broken home A family that is split up as a result of divorce, separation, or the desertion of one parent.

cluster suicides A series of suicides by several people in one area over a short period of time.

coma A state of unconsciousness.

copycat suicide A suicide that imitates one that occurred previously.

depression An intense feeling of unshakable gloom or sadness.

epidemic The rapid spread of a disease to a large number of people.

grief Extreme sadness or sorrow that develops after a crisis.

hormones Substances in the glands that help the body grow and stay healthy.

hot line A telephone line available in emergencies.

humiliation Shame; embarrassment.

media Television, radio, newspapers, magazines, and other forms of communication that reach many people.

mesmerized Fascinated.

overdose A dangerous and often fatal amount of drugs or alcohol.

peer pressure Force or strong demands by people of one's own age to behave in a certain way.

perfectionism An overriding desire to be perfect.

pessimism A negative view of the world; expecting the worst to happen.

psychiatrist A medical doctor who treats mental illness.

psychologist A person who is trained to study the mind and the way people behave.

self-destructive behavior Acting in a way that will harm oneself.

self-esteem Self-confidence; how a person feels about himself or herself.

sociologist A person who studies the behavior of groups and the ways in which people relate to one another.

subconscious A level of the mind in which thoughts and memories exist, but which people are not usually aware of.

subliminal Appealing to the subconscious mind rather than the conscious mind.

therapist A person trained to help a victim recover from an illness or accident.

will The power of the mind to control one's actions.

For Further Reading

Francis, Dorothy B. *Suicide: A Preventable Tragedy.* New York: E.P. Dutton, 1989.

Gardner, Sandra, with Rosenberg, Gary B., M.D. *Teenage Suicide.* New York: Julian Messner, 1985.

Hermes, Patricia. *A Time to Listen.* Orlando, FL: Harcourt Brace Jovanovich, 1987.

Kolehmaien, Janet. *Teen Suicide.* Minneapolis, MN: Lerner Publications, 1986.

Schleifer, Jay. *Everything You Need to Know About Teen Suicide.* New York: The Rosen Publishing Group, 1991.

Smith, Judie. *Coping with Suicide.* New York: The Rosen Publishing Group, 1990.

Where to Go for Help

National Suicide Hot Line (24 hours)
1-800-555-1212

Father Flanagan's Boys Town Hot Line
(for boys and girls) 1-800-448-3000

Youth Suicide National Center
1825 Eye Street, N.W.
Suite 400
Washington, D.C. 20006
(202) 429-2016

Teenage Suicide Center
3811 O'Hara Street
Pittsburgh, PA 15213
(412) 624-0719

National Institute of Mental
Health (NIMH)
5600 Fishers Lane
Room 17-99
Rockville, MD 20857
(301) 443-3673

Source Notes

Barish, Sidney. "Responding to Adolescent Suicide." *The Education Digest*, Jan. 1992, pp. 61–64.

Brower, M. "Lost Too Soon." *People Weekly*, May 21, 1990, pp. 56–59.

Hafen, Brent Q., and Frandsen, Kathryn J. *Youth Suicide, Depression and Loneliness.* Evergreen, CO: Cordillera Press, 1986.

Hermes, Patricia. *A Time to Listen.* Orlando, FL: Harcourt Brace Jovanovich, 1987.

Johnston, Jerry. *Why Suicide?* Nashville, TN: Oliver-Nelson Books, 1987.

Karlsberg, Elizabeth. "Teen Suicide." *Teen*, April 1991, pp. 24–29+.

Leder, Jane Mersky. *Dead Serious.* New York: Atheneum, 1987.

Smith, Judie. *Coping with Suicide.* New York: The Rosen Publishing Group, 1990.

Wartik, Nancy. "Jerry's Choice." *American Health*, Oct. 1991, pp. 73–76.

Index

American Association of
    Suicidology, 21, 23
Auschwitz death camp, 59

Belknap, Ray, 11

Caffrey, Dr. Thomas, 8
Copycat suicide. *See* Teen suicide.

Hendrix, Jimi, 15
Hot lines. *See* Suicide prevention.

Johnston, Jerry, 42
Judas Priest, 10, 11

Monroe, Marilyn, 15

National Institute on Alcohol Abuse
    and Alcoholism, 19
National Institute of Mental Health
    (NIMH), 7
Nazis, 59

Plano, Texas, 55
Prinze, Freddie, 15

Robinson, Todd, 27

Sheridan, Arkansas, 46
Stevens, Spencer, 15
Students Against Suicide, 46

Suicide counseling. *See* Hot lines,
    Suicide prevention.
Suicide prevention, 49–58
    counseling, 47, 55, 58
    hot lines, 62
    listening, 49–50, 51
    in school, 54–55

Teen suicide
    as copycat suicide, 37, 39
    and depression, 16–19
    and drug and alcohol use, 7, 19–21,
        32, 36
    and family life, 7, 24–26
    and the media, 9, 11
    and mental-health problems, 7
    methods, 35–37
    misconceptions, 33
    and personality, 13–16
    prevention. *See* Suicide prevention.
    and race, 13
    statistics, 5, 7, 13, 19, 21, 24, 27,
        29, 30, 45, 49
    survivor guilt, 44–45
    survivors, 42–47
    warning signs, 30–33

Vance, Jay, 11

Waterford, Helen, 59
Whitehead, Jerry Carr, 11
World War II, 59

Photo Credits